Gleanings Of 'the Robin Family' By A Robin [m. Robbins]. Private Ed. [with] Armorial Bearings Of The Robins Or Robbins Family Of England [and] Notes On The Armorial Bearings

Mills Robbins

GLEANINGS

OF

"THE ROBIN FAMILY,"

BY A ROBIN.

With Arms and Crests.

PRIVATE EDITION.

1880.

Ent. Sta. Hall.]

CONTENTS.

		PAGE
PREFACE	. . . . .	1
INTRODUCTION	. . . .	3
ITALY		
ROME	. . . . .	5
FRANCE	. . . . .	6
POICTOU AND ANJOU	. . .	12
BRETAGNE	. . . .	13
JERSEY	. . . . .	14
ENGLAND		
BUCKINGHAMSHIRE	. . .	17
CAMBRIDGESHIRE	. . .	19
KENT	. . . . .	20
OXFORDSHIRE	. . . .	21
GLOUCESTERSHIRE	. . .	23
CORNWALL	. . . .	30
WORCESTERSHIRE	. . .	35
LEICESTERSHIRE	. . .	36
NORFOLK	. . . .	38
SOMERSETSHIRE	. . .	40
HERTFORDSHIRE	. . .	43
DORSETSHIRE	. . . .	46
SUSSEX	. . . .	47
WILTSHIRE	. . . .	48
YORKSHIRE	. . . .	50
WARWICKSHIRE	. . .	51
HAMPSHIRE	. . . .	52
SURREY	. . . .	53
ESSEX	. . . .	54
CHESHIRE	. . . .	55
DEVONSHIRE	. . . .	57
STAFFORDSHIRE	. . .	58
WALES	. . . . .	59
ARMS UNKNOWN	. . .	60

PREFACE.

THE origin of this little work is the result of an attempt to trace as far back as possible the branch of the Robbins Family, of which I am a member. I had not proceeded very far before I found I was obliged to extend my researches more widely than I had intended.

Thinking, therefore, that these notes might be of some interest to other members of the Robin, Robins, or Robbins Family, I determined to publish a few copies of them merely for private circulation.

In doing so, I do not claim any special merit for my work, as I have not been able to obtain access to the wills of several families. Therefore the work must remain, to some extent, circumscribed.

I am greatly indebted to many members of the Family for the valuable information they have so kindly afforded me.

The other chief sources from which I have collected my notes have been the rent rolls from the close of the 12th century, and the hundred rolls of Edward I., &c., to which I obtained access in the Bodleian Library.

In any matter of doubt, I have had the kind assistance of my esteemed friend, the eminent historian and antiquary, Mr. James Parker, M.A., Oxon, son of Mr. John Henry Parker, C.B., F.S.A., M.A.

M. R.

ROCHESTER HOUSE, OXFORD.
1880.

INTRODUCTION.

THE Robin, sometimes Robins Family, are supposed to be descended from the ancient tribes of the Robini, who inhabited the district of Venaissin, in Italy, and from whom sprang the Counts de Robin, who lived at Rome in the 10th century.

Guy Robin was the founder of the Family in France in the beginning of the 13th century.

Payne, in his Armorial of Jersey, says: "This branch of the Family has been settled in the island from time immemorial."

The Family appears in England at the end of the 13th century, where the name is commonly spelt "Robyns" (y and i being frequently interchanged): "Robbins" does not appear till the end of the 15th century.

The Family appears in Wales in the 16th century, and in Ireland in the 17th.

ROME.

ARMS OF COUNT ROBIN OF ROME

ARMS.—Quarterly, gules and or, over all a fess or,
between three martlets sable, two and one.

CREST.—A key, or.

SUPPORTS.—Two savages.

MOTTO.—Pin forte nell' anversita.

The Counts de Robin lived at Rome in the
10th century in great éclat and splendour.

FRANCE.

I. GUY ROBIN, the founder of the family in France, took the Cross in order to accompany King Philip Augustus, in his expedition to the Holy Land : returning whence he died at Vienne, in Dauphiné, and was interred in a costly tomb, bearing the following epitaph :—

𝕮𝔶 : 𝔤𝔦𝔱 𝔩𝔦 𝔭𝔯𝔢𝔲𝔵 𝕮𝔥𝔢𝔟𝔞𝔩𝔦𝔢𝔯 𝕲𝔲𝔶 𝕽𝔬𝔟𝔦𝔫, 𝔡𝔦𝔱 𝔩𝔦 𝕴𝔱𝔞𝔩𝔦𝔢𝔫. 𝕻𝔯𝔦𝔢𝔷 𝔭𝔬𝔲𝔯 𝔩'𝔞𝔪𝔢 𝔡𝔢 𝔩𝔦. 1223.

(Here lies the noble Chevalier Guy Robin, surnamed the Italian. Pray for his soul. 1223.)

He left by Sigismund, de Curaciole de Saint Angelo, his wife :—

Hugues, who succeeded him.

Guillaume, who died without issue, so far as is known. (Is this the ancestor of Robin, of Jersey ?)

II. Hugues de Robin, married Leonore des Beaux, natural daughter of Raimond, the second of the name, Prince of Orange, by whom he had

François, who succeeded him, and

several daughters.

III. François de Robin, Chevalier, crossed into Africa in 1270, and by his will dated

1296, without mentioning his wife, named as his heir, Robert, who passed as his son.

IV. Robert de Robin, Damoiseau, married at Malancene, September 5th, 1321, Philipponette, daughter of the noble and powerful Rican de L'Espine, Lord of the said place and of Aulan, also of Philippine D'Arguison ; and in his will, dated March 20th, 1371, received by Rostang Costant, he named his son as his heir, and gave a legacy to his daughter with entail. He had by his marriage :—

> François, who succeeded him.
> Lucie, wife of Sabian (?) de Verone, Damoiseau, from the district of Vinsobre-en-Dauphiné.

V. François de Robin, the second of the name, surnamed the Wolf, being present at the battle of Poictiers, was near enough to King John to give him his horse, that of this Prince having just been wounded ; he served there with five esquires. He married September 1st, 1362, Marie, daughter of Raynaud de Beaumont (de Bellomonte), sister of Amblend (?), from whom is descended the famous Baron des Adrets. By his will dated 1397, we find that he left three children :—

> François, who succeeded him.
> Bertrandetta.

Rose, married to Gauteline de Sainte Yalle.

VI. François de Robin, the third of the name, Lord of Beaumont, &c., was made a Chevalier in the time of Crevant. Pope Eugenius IV., in consideration of the services that he had rendered the Church in prosecuting the heretics, and as being a descendant of some of the ancient inhabitants of Rome, by a bull declared him and his male descendants perpetual citizens of Rome. He married in 1411, Marie Durfort (in Latin, Duroforti), widow of the noble Jacques de Ganfridi de Malancene, by whom he had :—

> Pierre, who devoted himself to the study of medicine.
> Gaucher, who succeeded him.
> Beatrix, married to the Baron de St. Esteve.

VII. Gaucher de Robins, Chevalier, married, January 9th, 1443, Agnes, daughter of the noble Jean de Puy, from the branch of the family which founded the house of L'Espine. From this marriage came an only son.

VIII. Robert de Robins, Chevalier, heir by his father's will, dated 1467. He made an alliance with Cécile de Ganfridi, daughter of

Ebzear, Count and Baron of D'Entrechant, who had an only son.

IX. François de Robin, the fourth of the name, Chevalier, Lord of Châteauneuf, married February 5th, 1522, to Polisene de Bouvard, Dame de Saint André, daughter of Alexander Damoiseau. This marriage contract, drawn up by Matthieu Rabasse, a notary of Avignon, was ratified at Avignon in the Hotel de Claude de Torbin, in the presence of Pierre de Cambisand Antoine de Reumsat His children were :—

> Henri, died in Pologne, at the flight of the King.
> Theodore, killed at the Battle of Coutra, being a Cornet in a Company of Gendarmes.
> Paul, who succeeded him.

X. Paul de Robins, Chevalier, Count and Baron de Châteauneuf de Saint André, etc., joined the Counts of Suzet and Sourmerieve against the Protestants ; they created him Chevalier of the Order of the Golden (Milice?) and gave him permission to bear in his Arms a golden key as his Crest. He lost a leg at the Siege of Bréoute, in 1586, serving under the Duc D'Eperon. He had married Catherine de Mailles, and had by her :—

Pierre Etienne, who succeeded him.
Catherine Rose, died young.

XI. Pierre Etienne de Robins, the first of the name, Chevalier, Count and Baron de Châteauneuf de Saint André, etc; born January 19th, 1566, served under Kings Henry IV. and Louis XIII ; was dangerously wounded at the siege of Montauban. He made his will June 1st, 1627, before Martinelli, the notary, and died in his house at Malancene, January 9th, 1650, after having squandered the greater part of his property. He married Catherine Rose Dumas, and had by her :—

François, died without marrying.
Paul, who succeeded him.

XII. Paul de Robins, Chevalier, Lord D'Entrevon, born in 1623, was present at the Battle of Rordlinque, in Germany, and died October 5th, 1698, leaving by Anne de Martinelle his wife, the daughter of Jean :—

Pierre, who succeeded him.
Paul François, an Ecclesiastic.
Elizabeth Marguerite, died without marrying.

> Claudine, died without marrying.
>
> Anne, married to André Gunner.
>
> Madelene, the wife of Jean Baizet de St. Romain.
>
> Catherine, a nun.

XIII. Pierre de Robins, Chevalier, Lord D'Entrevon, married Marguerite du Ponte, by whom he had :—

XIV. François de Robin, the fifth of the name, Chevalier, Lord D'Entrevon, married to Gabrielle, daughter of Mari de Plantin, Lord of Villeperdrix, from whom are descended :—

> Pierre Etienne, who succeeded him, and a daughter, a nun.

XV. Pierre Etienne de Robins, the second of the name, Chevalier, Lord D'Entrevon married Madeline de Vitalis, by whom there remain the following living children :—

> Jean Joseph Xavier Antoine, whom some call the Count de Robins, a Captain in the Calvary.
>
> Joseph Antoine, an Ecclesiastic.

ARMS OF ROBIN DE LA TREMBLAGE, OF POICTOU
AND ANGOU.

ARMS.—Gules, two keys argent in saltire, in
chief an escallop argent, in the blanks three
escallops or, at the end of each a drop of
water ppr.

ARMS OF ROBIN OF BRETAGNE.

ARMS.—Gules, three bars argent, paleways.

Robin in Bretagne, in the province of Nantes, a noble, who sprang from Pierre Robin, the father of one of the most ancient families in Poictou, in 1360.

JERSEY.

ARMS OF ROBIN OF JERSEY.

ARMS.—Azure, a chev. gules, between three marigolds, closed or slipped and leaved ppr.

JERSEY.

In the year 1331 Raulin Robin was a land-owner in the parish of S. Brelade, and one of the jurymen thereof deputed to ascertain the Crown dues of the parish. Richard and Raulin Robin performed the same office for the parish of S. Laurence.

For several centuries a branch of the Robin family has resided at S. Brelade's, in the Church of which place may be found a number of monuments to the memory of the above family.

John Robin, Esq., who was elected Councillor of the Parliament of Paris, May 11th, 1618, bore the Arms of Jersey.

In 1716 Raulin Robins, Esq., was Lieutenant Bailey of Jersey.

In 1840 Charles Robin, Esq., left £2500 to the Hospital of S. Helier, which enabled the Trustees to build a Chapel for the Hospital, and to provide for the payment of a Chaplain. In the same year James Robin, Esq., was President of the Benefit Society for the Merchant Seamen of Jersey.

John Robin, Esq., of Bishop's Teignton, Devonshire, claims relation to the above family. He has in his posession a very ancient seal of the Arms of the Jersey family.

The Rev. P. R. Robin, M.A., Woodchurch Rectory, Birkenhead, also claims relation to the Jersey family.

ENGLAND.

BUCKINGHAMSHIRE.

ROGER ROBIN of Ravenston held of the Prior land in the year 1279.

In the year 1340, John-le-Rous, Richard Gladwyn, Hugh Robyns, and others, certified that the beans and peas were deficient in produce, by reason of the dry summer.

Fines were passed of lands in Bichendon over Winchendon and Waddesdon in the year 1346 between Hugh Robyns of Winchendon and Richard le Frankelyn and Agnes his wife, to whom they were conveyed with remainder to the heirs of Richard.

In the year 1468, John Robyns was presented to the Rectory of Thornton by Master Robert Ingleton.

From one of the Ashmole M.SS. there is a mention of an Adam Robyns who was a Fellow of Eton College in the year 1595.

c

In the Church of Langley Marsh on the pavement of Chancel is the following :

" Here lieth the body of Hannah, the wife of Thomas Robbins, of this Parish, Gentleman. She died July 25th, 1719, aged 72 years. Here also lieth the body of the above Thomas Robbins. He died February 12th, 1721, aged 65 years."

CAMBRIDGESHIRE.

FROM the Hundred Rolls of Edward I. we get the mention of a Margaret Robines in the year 1279.

KENT.

WE get the mention, in the year 1279, of Galfridus the son of Dera Robins, respecting a messuage of land, which the father of the then possessor had bought of Galfridus, who had inherited it from his mother Dera, who had it from the Priory of Bernewell.

A John Robins was Baron of Parliament for Dover in the first and fifth Parliament of Queen Elizabeth.

Thomas Robins was Rector of Otterden in the year 1682, and Vicar of Lenham in 1684. He died in 1701. He left £20 per annum to S. John's College, Cambridge, for the benefit of two Scholars, educated in the School. Francis Robins, M.A., son of Thomas and Vicar of Lenham, left in the year 1720, £3 per annum to the most industrious poor of Lenham, to be distributed by the Minister or Churchwardens on March 11th.

OXFORDSHIRE.

A JOHN ROBIN held a cottage in Dunstew in the year 1279.

A Walter Robyn, of Sypford, is mentioned in the same year.

William Robyns, Chaplain, was presented by the Abbot and Convent of Ensham to the Church of Sulthorn on May 18th, 1415.

William Masey quit claims to Robert James, Esq., Edmund Rede, John Faynel, Sen., and William Robyns, all his right in one toft and one virgate of land in Hedynton, which the said Robert and others had by the gift and feoffment of John Dalberd (Clerk), Robert Bruns, and John Hore, dated in Hedynton August 6th, 1418.

A John Robyns was Vicar of Ambrusden in the year 1510. He resigned the living December 31st, 1513.

In the reign of Henry VIII., John Robyns was Canon of Christ Church Cathedral, Oxford, and S. George's Chapel, Windsor.

In 1541, Thomas Hall, receiver of the temporalties of the Bishop of Lincoln to be paid on the Feast of S. Michael, received the sum of £77 12s. 3½d. from Richard Robyns and Thomas Barons of Banbury, who held certain lands or manors of the Bishop of Lincoln.

A George Robins was Mayor of Banbury in the year 1632; his son George was a mercer, and belonged to the Company of Mercers in the year 1669.

On the 16th of July, 1662, Thomas Robins, Mayor of Banbury, with nine Aldermen, all the six Capital Burgesses, and other officers of the Corporation, took oaths of allegiance and supremacy.

Thomas Robins is again mentioned in the year 1677.

GLOUCESTERSHIRE.

ARMS OF ROBYNS OR ROBBINS.

ARMS—Per pale, sable and argent, two flaunches and three fleur-de-lis in fess, all counter-changed.

CREST—Between two dolphins haurient respecting each other, or, a fleur-de-lis, per pale argent and sable.

MOTTO—Deus pro nobis, qui contra nos ?

GLOUCESTERSHIRE.

FROM the Subsidy Rolls of Gloucestershire
in the year 1327 we get the following names :
Robert Robyn, XIII. d.
Walter Robines, XV. d.g.
Richard Robines, XV. d. ob.

The Manor of Matson is pleasantly situated
on a Hill called Robin's Wood Hill (derived
from a wealthy family who lived here,) two
miles from the City of Gloucester.

In the year 1346, Edward III. granted it to
the Abbey of S. Peter, Gloucester. It was
held by Humphry de Bohun, Earl of Hereford,
and others.

In the year 1526, Abbot Parker granted a
lease of the Manor for seventy years to Thomas
Robins and Joan, his wife.

The Family of Robins continued to hold this
Manor as lessees after it had been allotted by
Henry VIII. to the Dean and Chapter of
Gloucester Cathedral as part of their endow-
ment. Members of this family appear on many
occasions subsequently as freeholders of Matson.

John the son of Thomas Robins took
possession of the Manor of Matson in the year

1553, and left it to his son Thomas, who married Joan, daughter of Lawrence Singleton, Esq., of Singleton Hall, Lancashire.

Richard Robins gave the Living of Matson to Lewis Crones in the year 1570.

Margaret, daughter of Thomas and Joan, married Jasper Selwyn, Esq., January 13th, 1591, at Kings Stanley, and as heiress brought him certain lands at Matson, in dowry.

Sir Ambrose Willoughby appears to have lived at Matson House about this time, for he is said to have built the present Manor House in the year 1594.

In the year 1597, Matson House passed into the hands of Jasper Selwyn, Esq., who married the heiress of Thomas Robins. But part of the Manor was still in possession of the Robins' Family, for in 1626 John Robins, by grant of the Dean and Chapter of Gloucester, gave the Living of Matson to William Ansell, M.A. He married Anne, daughter of William Stratford,[a] Esq., of Farmcote. She was buried in Matson Church May 11th, 1663, and until very lately the slab was to be seen in the Church.

The Rev. William Bazeley, M.A., the present Rector of Matson, in a paper read by him at

---

[a] Arms of Stratford—Barry of ten, over all a lion rampant.

Gloucester, January 25th, 1878, on the history of Matson, says :—

"It was during the time of William Selwyn, son of Jasper and Margaret, that Charles I. resided for twenty-six days at Matson House. (A Mr. Robins was living close by Matson House at this time.)

"Matson House has been little altered since that time, and it is easy to picture the White King, as he was called on account of his virtuous character, seated in the old dining hall, with the young princes, Charles and James, or joining his courtiers in his favourite game of bowls on the level green. Here was Chillingworth the divine, engaged in the most unclerical pursuit of making battering rams to demolish the city walls. Here also was Falkland, amiable, learned, and liberal beyond his age, lamenting the internecine strife, which was devastating the land and hindering the spread of knowledge. There are some marks on the window-sill of a room in the north-western gable, which tradition assigns to the swords of the young princes. Wraxall, in his memoirs, tells us that King James II. mentioned this feat to one of the Selwyns, amongst other recollections of Matson. The little Church was used for storing ammunition; and Charles, probably, made use of a room, now called the Chapel, for his daily devotions. The King's Chamber and Kitchen still retain their names. There are several letters extant which were written at this time from Matson House, one from the King begs the Marquis of Newcastle not to forget his 200 barrels of gunpowder. Tradition says that on the 5th of September, 1643, Charles and his sons rode sadly away down the lane, which leads by Snedham Green to Brookthorpe, then up across the fields to Sponebed Hill. It was whilst they were resting for a while at the ancient camp, called Kimsbury Castle or Castle Godwin, that one of the princes asked, 'When are we going home?' and he answered, 'Alas, my child, we have now no home to go to!'

"Jasper Selwyn died in 1634, and was buried at Matson. His monument describes him as 'Counsellor at law and one of His Majesty's Justices of Peace for the County of Gloucester.' From his will, which I have examined in the Gloucester Probate Court, it appears that he left his plate and other moveables to his daughters, Margaret, Sarah, and Dorothy, and certain fittings of the house, which he describes as 'wainscott and glass,' to his son William, stipulating that his widow, whom he makes his sole executrix, should have the use of them during her life-time. The will is a very short one, and more than half of it is a solemn declaration of his Christian faith. Margaret Selwyn survived her husband only two years."

William Robins, of Crum Hall, married Dorothy, daughter of Thomas Bacon, Esq., of Mansell, Somerset. She died May 26th, 1732, and was buried at Matson. William was the grandson of John and Anne Robins, and was a freeholder in Matson in 1734. He was High Sheriff for Gloucester in 1738.

As late as 1790, George Augustus Selwyn,[b] Esq., possessed the Manor of Matson. He made several alterations in the old family mansion of the Robins'. It is recorded that the original entrance to the mansion was an old-fashioned doorway, with heavy folding gates, thickly studded with nails, which opened into a courtyard, and was the principal entrance to Matson House.

On the 18th of January, 1603, Henry Robins was elected Town Clerk of Gloucester. It is recorded that he lived to a great age, and is

[b] Arms of Selwyn—Argent, on a bend cottised sable, three annulets or, within a bordure gules.

buried in the north transept of the Cathedral.
Upon his tomb is the following inscription :

" Here lieth the body of Henry Robins, Esq.,
who departed this life the 11th day of November, 1613."

And on a brass plate on the same tomb is
the following :

" Causidicus fueram, dum me mea fata sinebant
    Nunc mea stellifero causa peracta foro est.
Tristes et indignor tu (cui licet) argue causas
    O! quanto mitior sors mea sorte tua est."

Henry Robins and Daniel Lysons were
Sheriffs of the City of Gloucester in the year
1650.

Henry Robins was buried in the north
transept of the Cathedral, May 8th, 1653.

George Augustus Robbins, Esq., of Clay
Hill House Estate, near Lechlade, claims
relation to the before mentioned " Robins "
of Matson. This estate has been in the possession of this family for nearly 100 years.

Captain Spencer Percival Robbins and the
late General Pitt Robbins are brothers to the
above George Augustus.

NOTE.—With exception of names under date of 1327, all
are of the same family. I have not inserted pedigree of this
family, it being so incomplete : for Arms see front page.

CORNWALL.

ARMS OF ROBYNS OR ROBINS.

ARMS—ᶜParty per pale, argent and azure, a fess nebulée, between three robins all counter-changed.

MOTTO—Dives qui contentus.

CREST————————

ARMS—Quarterly nebulée, argent and azure four robins counterchanged.

ARMS—Or, on a bend argent, three pheons of the field, a crescent for a difference.

ᶜ A copy of these Arms was found in one of the Ashmole MSS. 1137, fol. 122, dating about the year 1600.

CORNWALL.

JOHN ROBYN held land in the Parishes of Tregemynyon, Trenewen, Crostover, Trego-seal, Keywyn and Bosvyon in the reign of Edward III.

Otto Robyns was Mayor of Bodmin in the year 1473.

Thomas Robyns of Trewardale bought land in the year 1581. The property remained vested in the Robyns Family until the end of the 17th century, when it was sold by Robert Robyns.

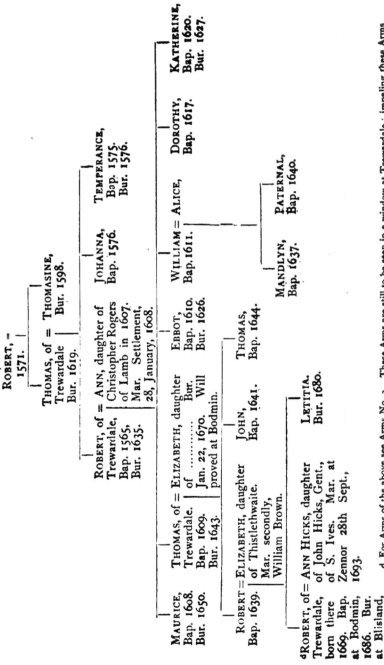

JOHN ROBYNS = JOHANNA.
Bur. 1544. | Bur. 1560.

ROBERT, = 1571.

THOMAS, of = THOMASINE,
Trewardale   Bur. 1598.
Bur. 1619.

ROBERT, of = ANN, daughter of Christopher Rogers of Lamb in 1607. Mar. Settlement, 28, January, 1608.
Trewardale, Bap. 1565, Bur. 1635.

JOHANNA, Bap. 1576.

TEMPERANCE, Bap. 1575. Bur. 1576.

THOMAS, of = ELIZABETH, daughter of .... Jan. 22, 1670. Will proved at Bodmin.
Trewardale. Bap. 1609. Bur. 1643.

EBBOT, Bap. 1610. Bur. 1626.

WILLIAM = ALICE,
Bap. 1611.

DOROTHY, Bap. 1617.

KATHERINE, Bap. 1620. Bur. 1627.

MANDLYN, Bap. 1637.

PATERNAL, Bap. 1640.

THOMAS, Bap. 1644.

MAURICE, Bap. 1608. Bur. 1650.

ROBERT = ELIZABETH, daughter of Thistlethwaite. Mar. secondly, William Brown.
Bap. 1639.

JOHN, Bap. 1641.

LETITIA. Bur. 1680.

4 ROBERT, of Trewardale, born there 1669. Bap. at Bodmin, 1686. Bur. at Blisland, 1711. = ANN HICKS, daughter of John Hicks, Gent., of S. Ives. Mar. at Zennor 28th Sept., 1693.

d For Arms of the above see Arms No. 3. These Arms are still to be seen in a window at Trewardale; impaling these Arms are,—three lions rampant, ducally crowned.

A Robyns, in the year 1620, married Alice, daughter of Henry Maynard, Esq., of Milton, Devonshire.

William Robyns was Mayor of Bodmin in the year 1627.

John Cavell of Trehaverock, married Jane Robins in the year 1628, at S. Mabyn.

Richard Vivian of S. Collomb, married Grace Robins at S. Mervyn, June 8th, 1631.

Richard ———— married Jane Robins in the year 1654, at S. Winnow.

John Robins married Jane Williams of Trevro, Oct. 1st, 1655, at Tywardreath.

• Sir Viel Vyvyan of Trelowarren, married Thomasine, daughter of James Robins, Gentleman, June 30th, 1671, at Constantine.

The Manor of Treguitha S. Hilary, was for some time in the possession of the Robins' family. They sold part of it in the year 1706.

ᶠ Stephen Robins, Esq., was Sheriff of Cornwall in the year 1701. S. Winnow was for some time in his possession. He was buried in the Church there, Feb. 25th, 1720.

ᵉ Arms of Vyvyan—Argent, a lion rampant gules, armed sable; Crest, a horse passant furnished ppr.

ᶠ For Arms, see No. 2.

D

· William Green married Frances Robins at S. Winnow in the year 1703.

The Barton of Tregenna, S. Ewe, was for many years held by the Robins family. The family is now represented at S. Ewe by a family named the Hopes.

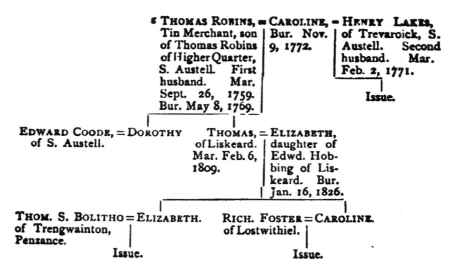

A Mr. Robins by his will bearing date 1768, gave the interest of Stock, amounting to nearly £7 per annum, for the support of a School in the parish of S. Burdock.

ᵉ This pedigree appears to be a part of that on page 32, but I have failed to connect it.

WORCESTERSHIRE.

A Thomas Robyns of Worcester is mentioned in the calendar of Escheat Rolls in the "Tower" in the reign of Edward III.

LEICESTERSHIRE.

IN the year 1337 a messuage and bovate of land in Frisby were given to the Prior and Convent of Laund by John Robyn of Ashfordby and Alice Buchand.

From a list of the freeholders of Osgathorpe, a place five miles north-east of Ashby-de-la-Zouch, we get the name of William Robins in the year 1630.

In the Church of Markfield on the floor of the nave is the following :

"Here lyeth the body of Dorothy Robins, wife of William Robins, of Osgathorpe, Gentleman. She died in 1708, aged 67 years."

"Here lieth the body of Thomas Avery, Gentleman, who married Dorothy, the only daughter of William Robins of Osgathorpe, by whom he left issue, one son and three daughters. He departed this life May 27th, 1705, aged 33 years."

"Here lieth interred in the same grave, Dorothy, the relict of the said Thomas Avery. She died November 3rd, 1731, aged 56 years."

Edward Willis, Lieutenant in the 37th Regiment of Infantry, son of Richard Willis, Esq., of Halsnead Park, married Harriette, daughter and co-heiress of the late Lieutenant-Colonel Robbins, May 12th, 1831.

NORFOLK.

SIR WILLIAM ROBYNS was Rector of SS. Peter and Paul's, Wramplingham, in the year 1448.

Sir Thomas Robyn possessed land in Stifkey in the year 1514.

In Tanner's M.SS. there is a letter from Henry Davy and John Robins, Bailiffs of Yarmouth, to Bishop Wren, denying the claims of Miles Hull, the Parish Clerk, March 26th, 1638.

From the memorials in the churchyard at Itteringham we get the names of—

THOMAS ROBINS.
Bur. 1726.
MARY, his wife.
Bur. 1725.

THOMAS ROBINS.
Bur. 1732.
MARY, his wife,
Widow of Rev. J. Fletcher,
and daughter of — Jefferies.
Bur. 1747.

[b] Richard Robins, Esq., was Lord of Mower's Hall Manor, Itteringham, in the year 1769. He had it from his father William, who had it from his uncle, Richard Robins.

A—Robins, Esq., also possessed the Manor of Bintre in the year 1769.

---

[h] This Manor is held of the Crown at 3s. 6d. per annum.

SOMERSETSHIRE.

ARMS OF ROBYNS OR ROBBINS.

ARMS—Per pale, sable and argent, two flaunches, and three fleur-de-lis in fess, all counterchanged.

CREST—Between two dolphins haurient respecting each other, or, a fleur-de-lis per pale argent and sable.

MOTTO—Esse quam videri.

SOMERSETSHIRE.

A JOHN ROBYNS, of the same family as
"Robyns" of Matson, was Mayor of Bristol in
the reign of Henry VI. One of his descendants was a -—— Robbins, of Crewherne,
whose son was Thomas Robbins, of Pillwell
Park, Hants. The latter had three sons :—

1. The late General Thomas Robbins, of Castle
   Malwood, Hants, who whilst in the 11th
   Hussars, distinguished himself in the
   famous charge of Waterloo, and after-
   wards exchanged into the Guards.

2. John Robbins, of Batramsley, Hants. His
   son, the Rev. John Robbins, D.D., was
   educated at Eton and Christ Church,
   Oxford; M.A., 1856; made D.D., Oxon,
   1868; is now Vicar of S. Peter's, Bayswater.
   He inherited the Batramsley estate, but
   sold it some years since.

3. The late Major Robbins, of Forest Lodge,
   near Southampton, who belonged to the
   17th Lancers.

Benjamin Robins, who was renowned for his great genius as a Mathematician, was born at Bath, in the year 1707.

A Rev. —— Robbins, D.D., was Rector of South Petherton, in 1789.

HERTFORDSHIRE.

ARMS OF ROBINS.

ARMS —[1]Gules, two fleur-de-lis each divided pale-ways and fastened to the sides of the escutcheon, the points following each other, or.

CREST—On a wreath a Talbot's Head, argent.

[1] A Robins bearing these Arms lived in London in the year 1633.

HERTFORDSHIRE.

JOHN ROBYNS was instituted to the living of S. Mary's, Stocking, Pelham, Nov. 14th, 1439, which was presented to him by Henry Hert, the patron. He resigned the living in the year 1443.

In the Church of S. Stephen, within S. Alban's, in the Chapel, south of the Church, on the floor, is the brass of a man in armour, and his wife, four sons and six daughters. The inscription is gone but in the Register is the following :—

"𝕳𝖎𝖈 𝖏𝖆𝖈𝖊𝖙 𝖂𝖎𝖑𝖑𝖎𝖊𝖑𝖒𝖚𝖘 𝕽𝖔𝖇𝖎𝖓𝖘, 𝕬𝖗𝖒𝖎𝖌𝖊𝖙, 𝖓𝖚𝖕𝖊𝖗 𝖈𝖑𝖊𝖗𝖎𝖈𝖚𝖘 𝖘𝖎𝖌𝖓𝖊𝖙𝖎 𝕰𝖉𝖜𝖆𝖗𝖉𝖎 𝖖𝖚𝖆𝖗𝖙𝖎 𝖓𝖚𝖕𝖊𝖗 𝖗𝖊𝖌𝖎𝖘 𝕬𝖓𝖌𝖑𝖎𝖘𝖊, 𝕶𝖆𝖙𝖍𝖊𝖗𝖎𝖓𝖆 𝖚𝖝𝖔𝖗 𝖊𝖏𝖚𝖘𝖉𝖊𝖒 𝖂𝖎𝖑𝖑𝖎𝖊𝖑𝖒𝖎 𝖊𝖙 𝖖𝖚𝖎 𝖖𝖚𝖎𝖉𝖊𝖒 𝖂𝖎𝖑𝖑𝖎𝖊𝖑𝖒𝖚𝖘 𝖔𝖇𝖎𝖎𝖙 4ᵗᵒ 𝖉𝖎𝖊 𝖒𝖊𝖓𝖘𝖎𝖘 𝕹𝖔𝖛𝖊𝖒𝖇𝖗𝖎𝖘 𝕬𝖓. 𝕯𝖔𝖒. 1482, 𝖖𝖚𝖆𝖗𝖚𝖒 𝖆𝖓𝖎𝖒𝖆𝖇𝖚𝖘, &𝖈."

Thomas Clotterbooke, clothier, of King's Stanley, married thirdly Joan, the daughter of John Robins, in the year 1610; no family by his third wife.

[k] In Norshaw Church, on the floor, is the following :—

"Here lyeth interred the body of Helen

[k] The Arms of this family are already given.

Arms of Boulton : A Hawk belled. Crest—on a wreath a Hawk belled.

Robins, wife of Elisha Robins, mercer, daughter
of William Boulton, Esqre., who departed this
life the 31st day of March, 1647, aged 32
years."

In the Churchyard of S. Mary's, Hertingford-
bury, several of the Robins' family are buried.
Date about 1700.

Thomas Robins was Mayor of S. Alban's
in 1717 and in 1728.

In the middle aisle of the Church of Royston
is the following :—

" Here lieth the body of Ann Robins; she
died June 1st, 1761, aged 47 years."

In the Church of S. James, Bushey, a tablet
records a George Manners Robins. He died
June 18th, 1865.

In the Church of S. Helen, Wheathamstead, a
marble cross is erected to the memory of Helen,
the wife of George Upton Robins. She died
January 15th, 1875, aged 54 years.

DORSETSHIRE.

SIR JOHN HODY, of Pillesdon, Knight and Chief Justice of England, left by will dated the year 1441 :—

Item lego William Robynys vj^s viij^d.
Item lego Richard Robyns iij^s iiij^d.

SUSSEX.

RADUS ROBYNES was Rector of Rede in the reign of Henry VIII.

WILTSHIRE.

Richard Robins of Ashton Keynes, Gentleman, was a Freeholder in the year 1539.

From the Muster Rolls of Wiltshire in the year 1539 we get the following :—

MALMESBURY.

"Robert Robyns, Archers viij.

John Robyns, Archers viij.

HIGHWORTH.

Thomas Robyns, a bill.

William Robyns, harnes, bowe, scheffe of arrowes, swerde and dagger.

Walter Robyns, a harnes, bill, sewered and daggar."

[1] A William Robins lived at Wilcott in the year 1587.

Henry Robbins possessed land near Woodborough in the year 1687, and was Churchwarden of Woodborough in the year 1691.

Several members of the Robbins family are buried in the churchyard of S. Mary Magdalen,

---

[1] From this date we get several names from the Church Registers at Wilcott, but a great gap appears in the Commonwealth, so that I have not been able to connect them.

Woodborough. There are also monumental inscriptions to the same family in the church.

William Robins succeeded Joseph Adye as Sheriff of Malmesbury in the year 1685, and continued Sheriff in the following year.

John Robins was elected Mayor of Salisbury in the year 1729, and re-elected in the year 1730.

A—Robins of Broughton, married Hester, third daughter of John Bythesea, Esq. of Week House, about the year 1730.

YORKSHIRE.

A JOHN ROBYNS was Vicar of Baffen in the
reign of Henry VIII.

WARWICKSHIRE.

A JOHN ROBYNS lived at Framton in the reign of Edward VI.

Silvester Robins of Warwick married the widow of Richard Bludd in the year 16—.

Roland Robins, Esq., of Pillaton, married Margaret, third daughter of John Woodward, of Avon-Dasset, in the year 16—.

A Robins, of Etington, married Johanna Fulwood in 16—.

^m Richard Robins, Esq., was a Member of the Town Council of Coventry, Aug. 27th, 1619. A member of this family carried on great trade as a Wool Stapler about this time, and a small estate is still in possession of a descendant of the family.

J. Yeoman Robins, Esq., of Myton House, Warwick, son of the late J. Robins, Esq., is related to the above.

The Rev. Thomas Robins, of Strelton, completed his studies for the Church under Dr. Doddridge in the year 1756. He died in March, 1810, in his 78th year.

^m For Arms see Gloucestershire.

HAMPSHIRE.

A FRANCIS ROBINS was a Burgess of Portsmouth, in the year 1557.

In the time of Queen Elizabeth, we find a strange controversy recorded :—

Edward Robins, the Rector of Minstead, and John Sharpwell, touching a bond which Robins the plaintiff had given Sharpwell, for payment of first fruits, due from the benefice in the time of John Dysley, predecessor of John Robins in the Rectory.

SURREY.

A JOHN SCOT, Esq., married, first, Elizabeth, daughter of William Robins, Merchant of the Staple of Calais in the year 1540. He died August 15th. 1558, and was buried in the Chapel of Our Lady in the Church of S. Giles, Camberwell.

In the wall of south aisle of this Church, is a monument of two arches, in which are the figures of an old man in a gown, another in armour, and a woman between. On a black marble slab is the following :—

"John Scot," Lord of the Manor of Camberwell (ye son and heire of John Scot, Sheriff of Surrey and Sussex in ye year 1520, one of ye Barons of Exchequer) in ye year 1548, being married to Elsabe ye daughter and heiress of John Robyns of London, Merchant of the Staple at Calais, by whom he had issue, John, Richard, Edward, William, Bartholomew, and Acton."

ESSEX.

THOMAS GENT, ESQ. of Moyno Park, Counseller to Edward de Vere, Earl of Oxford, and held in high estimation by Queen Elizabeth for his learning, married secondly. in the year 1586, Elizabeth, sister of a Morgan Robyns, Esq., and widow of Robert Hogeson, Esq. of London. No family by his second wife.

CHESHIRE.

ARMS OF ROBIN.

ARMS.—Az. on a chev. or, three thistles, ppr.

CREST.—A robin, ppr.

MOTTO.—" Vivit post funera virtus."

CHESHIRE.

JAMES KELSALL, ESQ. of Cheadle, married Ann Robyn, Feb. 12th, 1593, at Peele; she was a daughter of — Golborne, Esq., of Golborne.

A Robins possessed part of the Manor of Tytherington Hall, near Macclesfield, in the year 1670.

n Arms of Kelsall family: Ermine, a bend engrailed sable.

o Arms of Robin, already given.

DEVONSHIRE.

[p] THOMAS ROBINS, ESQ., of Bratton Clovelly, in the reign of Queen Ann, is reported to be a representative of a branch of the Robins family of antiquity and importance in the county at the time the Visitation took place of families bearing arms. They disclaimed them either to avoid expense or to enter pedigree.

The Robins of Venu Hall, Taverstock, and some other parts of Devon, are of this family.

[q] Edward Cookworthy Robins, Esq., F.R.I.B.A., F.S.A., Tower House, S. John's Wood, London, is also of this family. His great-grandfather was a native of Plymouth.

[p] For Arms, see No. 1 Cornwall.

[q] It is recorded of this family, that an ancient relic, which for many generations was in possession of the family, in the shape of a gold seal ring, on which were the Arms of the family. This relic had been presented by the Government to an ancestor of the same, for some meritorious exploit or service rendered to the country. It had descended to Thomas Robins, Esq., of London, at whose death it was sought for, but could not be found.

STAFFORDSHIRE. .

r JOHN ROBINS, gentleman, was returned Member of Parliament for the Borough of Stafford, in the year 1748. He died in November, 1754.

r For Arms, see Gloucestershire.

WALES.

ROBERT ap. Hol. ap. ROBYN lived at S. Asaph in the reign of Henry VIII.

Master John Robyns was Canon and Prebend in the Cathedral Church of Bangor. The said John Robyns was also Vicar of the Parish Church of S. Beblick, and of the Moore Chappell of Caern, in the Deanery of Arvon, in the reign of Henry VIII.

John Robins was Vicar of Llanbeblie, in the Diocese of Bangor, in the reign of Henry VIII. This is probably the same person as the one mentioned in the preceding paragraph.

Arms of Robyns.

* **Arms**.—Per fesse, indented, argent and azure,
a fesse, indented, counterchanged ; in chief
two escallops of the second.

* It is not known to which family these Arms belong.

SUBSCRIBERS.

LANE, Mrs. E., Honeystreet, Wilts.

ROBIN, J. Esq., Bishop's Teignton, Devon.

ROBIN, Rev. P. R., M.A., Woodchurch Rectory, Birkenhead (2 copies).

ROBINS, B., Esq., Lords' Wood Road, Beech Lanes,. Nr. Birmingham.

ROBINS, B. S., Esq., 122, High Street, Bordesley, Birmingham.

ROBINS, E. C., Esq., F. R. I. B. A., F. S. A., London (6 copies).

ROBINS, E. W., Esq., West Hill Lodge, Brighton.

ROBINS, J., Esq., 6, King's Bench Walk, Temple, London.

ROBINS, J. J., Esq., North Street, Derby.

ROBINS, J. W., Esq., 16, Hervey Road, Shooter's Hill Road, London.

ROBINS, J. W., Esq., S. Ann's Road, Tottenham, London.

ROBINS, S. W., Esq.. The Rookery, Stevenage, Herts.

ROBINS, S. W., Esq., 70, Tyrwhitt Road, New Cross, London.

ROBINS, Rev. W. H., M.A., Gillingham Vicarage, Kent.

ROBINS, Mrs., The Elms, Watford, Herts (2 copies).

ROBBINS, Miss A., Shropham Vicarage, Norfolk (2 copies).

ROBBINS, A. J. F., Esq., 37, Lorrimore Square, London.

ROBBINS, C., Esq., Eastcot, Weston-super-Mare.

ROBBINS, C., Esq., 1, Lincoln's Inn, London.

ROBBINS, Miss E., Victoria House, S. Mary's Hill, Newbury.

ROBBINS, E., Esq., The Limes, Moulsham, Chelmsford.

ROBBINS, E. V., Esq., New Church Road, Camberwell, Surrey.

ROBBINS, G. A., Esq., Clay Hill House, Lechlade, Gloucester.

ROBBINS, H., Esq., 23, Church Road, Willesden, London.

ROBBINS, H., Esq.. Northfield, Witney, Oxon.

ROBBINS, J., Esq., The Hill, Buiford, Wilts.

ROBBINS, Rev. J., D.D., Kensington Park Road, London (2 copies).

ROBBINS, R., Esq., The Hollies, Kenilworth.

ROBBINS, Captain S. P., 5, James' Street, London.

ROBBINS, W., Esq., The Hawthorns, Small Heath, Nr. Birmingham.

A. R. MOWBRAY AND CO., PRINTERS, OXFORD.

Armorial Bearings
the Robins or Robbins Family
of England

.

No. 1.—Cornwall.

No. 1.—Arms—Party per pale, argent and azure, a fess nebulée, between three robins all counterchanged.

Crest—A tilting spear erect, two marshal batons in saltire, banded with a riband in fess nebulée.

Motto—Dives qui contentus.

No. 2.—Arms—Quarterly nebulée, argent and azure, four robins counterchanged.

No. 3.—Arms—Or, on a bend argent, three pheons of the field.

No. 4.—Gloucestershire.

No. 4.—Arms—Per pale, sable and argent, two flaunches, and three fleur-de-lis in fess, all counterchanged.

Crest—Between two dolphins haurient respecting each other, or, a fleur-de-lis per pale, argent, and sable.

Mottos—Deus pro nobis, quis contra nos? and Esse quam videri.

No. 5.—Hertfordshire.

ules, two fleur-de-lis, each divided paleways

d fastened to the sides of the escutcheon, the

ints following each other or.

talbot's head, argent.

ursu nunquam deficiens.

No. 6.—Unknown.

er fesse, indented, argent and azure; a fesse,

dented, counterchanged; in chief, two escal-

ops of the second.

Notes on the Armorial Bearings of the Robins or Robbins Family of England.

THE accompanying engraving of a late Tudor window, contains in the upper lights all the Arms belonging to the Robins, or Robbins Family of England, blazoned in their proper colours. They will be found in the same order as in the "Gleanings," with the exception of the Cornish Arms, which are supposed to be the oldest. "Clark, in his Introduction to Heraldry," speaking of canting or allusive arms, says, "There can scarcely be a greater proof of their antiquity." When speaking of the Cornish Arms as being the oldest, No. 6 is not intended to be included.

No. 1.—The earliest mention I have been able to obtain of this Coat is on the shield of the Scot or Scott Family, see Ashmole MSS. 1137, fol. 122, Bodleian Library, the same Family as mentioned in "Gleanings," page 53, which records the marriage, 1548.

No. 2.—Is the Coat borne by Stephen Robins, of S. Winnow, Sheriff of Cornwall, 1701.

No. 3.—Is the Coat of Robert Robins, mentioned in "Gleanings," page 32, but the authority is somewhat doubtful. It is the Coat of Thistlethwaite his grandfather, from whom he inherited Trewardale. I assume he adopted the Arms of his grandfather and grandmother. Impaling these Arms are, gules, three lions rampant, argent, ducally crowned; or. See Maclean's History of Trigg Minor, page 45.

No. 4.—For copy of this Coat see "Harleian MSS. Visitation of Gloucestershire, Selwyn Pedigree," British Museum. The marriage took place in 1591, and is recorded in "Gleanings," page 25.

No. 5.—A. Robins, of London, bore this Coat, 1633. "Edmonson's Heraldry," British Museum.

No. 6.—The College of Heralds has been searched, but they are unable to give any clue to what branch or county this Coat belongs; but say, "from its simplicity it is undoubtedly very old."

ADDITIONS.

The Cornwall Crest and Hertfordshire Motto have been received from members of the Family.

ERRATA.

The Arms under Cheshire in the "Gleanings" are a repetition of the Arms of Jersey, a member of that Family having resided there. In the above mistake I was misled by "Burke's General Armory," which also gives the wrong description. For correct read,—

Arms—Azure, a chev, gules, between three marigolds, closed or slipped and leaved ppr.

Crest—A chough.

Motto—" Vivit post funera virtus."

NOTE.—The above description was received from J. Robin, Esq., Bishop Teignmouth, Devon, in whose family these Arms have been used for many years.

CPSIA information can be obtained at www.ICGtesting.com
Printed in the USA
BVOW07s1411280314

349104BV00009B/205/P